THE HUMAN EQUATION: ORIGINS

ALSO BY KEVIN A. STARLINGS

The Kourage Trilogy
A memoir series about rhythm, resilience, and redemption.

The Manual They Never Gave Us
A parenting blueprint for the real world.

Educate In Color™ Collection
A body of work examining education, power, endurance, and structural harm.

— *When Numb Becomes Normal*
— *Taught to Endure*
— *Our Oppressor Will Never Educate Our Children*
— *The Way Out Had a Beat*
— *Infrastructure, Not Enrichment*
— *They Were Never Failing — The System Is*

The Human Equation Series
A systems-level blueprint for transforming education.

The Human Work Series
Soul-centered guides for the people who do the work.

The Human
Equation: Origins

Transforming Wellness Into Equity

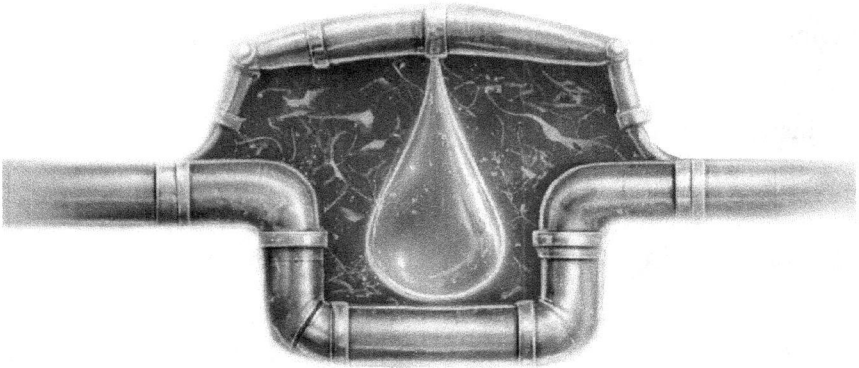

By
Kevin A. Starlings

The Human Equation: Origins
Copyright © 2026 by Kevin A. Starlings
All rights reserved.

Published by The Starlings Foundation Press

This book is part of a growing body of work committed to examining how educational systems shape human capacity, dignity, and opportunity. It explores how learning is influenced not only by instruction, but by the physical, emotional, and environmental conditions in which education takes place.

The content reflects lived experience, research-informed practice, and professional insight intended to support capacity-building learning, dialogue, and critical reflection across educational, community, and policy contexts.

The materials presented are intended for educational, informational, and reflective purposes only. They are not a substitute for professional judgment or the guidance of qualified professionals in education, healthcare, mental health, legal, or other fields. Readers are encouraged to consider their own contexts and consult appropriate professionals when making decisions related to personal, familial, educational, or organizational circumstances.

This work affirms the complexity of human experience and recognizes that no single approach is effective for every individual, family, classroom, or community.

ISBNs:

Paperback: 979-8-9946923-5-6
Ebook: 979-8-9946923-3-2

First Edition
Printed in the United States of America

TABLE OF CONTENTS

PART I

The Moment Before the Movement

PART II

The Pattern

PART III

The Pilot

PART IV

The Science Beneath the Story

PART V
The Origin of Equity

PART VI
The Rise of a Model

PART VII
The Turn Toward the Future

PART VIII
The Beginning

AUTHOR'S NOTE

The stories, observations, and systems described in this book are real.

The names are not.

Throughout *The Human Equation: ORIGINS*, I have intentionally anonymized schools, districts, organizations, initiatives, and geographic identifiers. This decision was not made to obscure the truth, but to protect it.

The conditions examined in these pages are not unique to one school, one city, or one institution. They are systemic. They are patterned. And they appear, with remarkable consistency, wherever children are asked to learn in environments that have not been designed to capacity-building their bodies, nervous systems, or dignity.

By removing identifying details, this book shifts the focus away from attribution and toward architecture—from who did what, to how systems behave. Anonymization allows the reader to engage with the underlying dynamics without distraction, defensiveness, or regional framing. It ensures that the work can be read not as a case study of a single place, but as a mirror reflecting conditions present in many places at once.

All characters represented are composites. All settings are contextualized rather than named. Any resemblance to specific institutions is not incidental—it is structural.

This choice also reflects an ethical commitment. The purpose of this work is not exposure, blame, or institutional critique for its own sake. It is to surface the often-invisible conditions that shape learning, behavior, and equity, and to offer language for addressing them at scale.

The frameworks introduced in this book—the Human Equation, the Flow Model, the Condition Equation, and the Five Wells of Student Wellness—are grounded in lived experience, research-informed practice, and direct observation. They are offered not as commentary on any one system, but as tools for reimagining systems everywhere.

The truth does not require names to be accurate.

Sometimes, removing them allows the truth to be seen more clearly.

A NOTE FOR READERS

This book is written at the intersection of story, systems, and science.

The Human Equation: ORIGINS is not a traditional education book. It is not a policy manual, a research report, or a collection of best practices—though it is informed by all three. It is a work of narrative nonfiction that traces how conditions shape capacity, how capacity shapes behavior, and how behavior shapes learning long before outcomes ever appear.

The stories in these pages are drawn from real environments and lived experience, but they are intentionally anonymized and often composite in nature. The purpose is not to document a single school, district, or city, but to surface patterns that repeat across many systems. Readers are encouraged to see not *where* this happened, but *how* it happens—again and again—whenever human needs are treated as secondary to institutional demands.

This book introduces several core frameworks—the Human Equation, the Flow Model, the Condition Equation, and the Five Wells of Student Wellness—not as abstract theories, but as language for realities educators, students, and families already live every day. These frameworks are meant to help readers name what has long been felt but rarely articulated: that learning is not only cognitive, but physiological; not only instructional, but environmental; not only individual, but systemic.

You do not need a background in education, neuroscience, or policy to read this book. You only need a willingness to consider that bodies enter classrooms before minds do, and that systems reveal their values through the conditions they create—or allow to persist.

ORIGINS is the first book in a larger arc. It is the excavation—the careful uncovering of truths beneath tradition, habit, and assumption. It does not attempt to solve every problem it names. Instead, it focuses on clarity: understanding where inequity begins, how wellness becomes infrastructure, and why reform efforts so often fail when they ignore the human foundations of learning.

Later books will ask different questions. This one asks only the first—and most essential—one:

What if the work of equity begins not with outcomes, but with conditions?

Read slowly. Read reflectively. And read with the understanding that if parts of this book feel familiar, uncomfortable, or uncannily recognizable, that recognition is not accidental.

It is the point.

INTRODUCTION

Before We Named the Movement

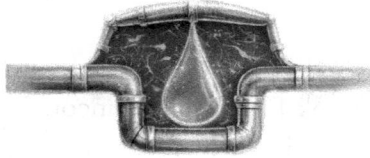

He stood there longer than a child should ever have to stand—silent, waiting for water that would not come.

The hallway was already warm, the early-morning kind of warm that settled into old buildings before the sun fully rose. The metal of the fountain was cool against his fingertips, but the spout stayed dry. He pressed the button once. Twice. A third time, as if the building might give in out of mercy.

Nothing.

He looked around, not for help, but for witnesses. Children learn early which disappointments are worth reporting and which ones the world has already decided to ignore. This was the second kind. His lips were cracked. His backpack sagged. He wiped his mouth with the back of his hand and walked away, carrying a thirst the adults in his life had long stopped noticing.

That moment—quiet, ordinary, easy to miss—was the moment the movement began.

I didn't call it a movement then.

I didn't even call it a project.

I just knew something was wrong.

A child should not begin his day dehydrated before he ever sits down to learn.

A classroom should not run on fumes before it runs on hope.

A school should not ration care like it's a privilege.

But for years, we treated the smallest failures as normal. We stepped over broken fountains, carried cases of bottled water to classrooms, scribbled "out of order" signs that hung there so long they became part of the décor. We spoke about equity in boardrooms while the most basic form of dignity—clean, cold water—remained inconsistent at best, inaccessible at worst.

Nobody meant to overlook hydration. That's the dangerous thing about inequity: it rarely announces itself as cruelty. It arrives as inconvenience, then lingers as inevitability.

I had been in countless classrooms before that morning. I'd sat with teachers who did everything but open their own veins to pour into their students. I'd watched school leaders stretch budgets so thin they could see the other side. I'd listened to parents explain that their children were doing their best, even when the system was not.

And still, I had missed the weight of that moment—the boy, the fountain, the quiet surrender—until the pattern began repeating itself like a whisper I could no longer ignore.

It wasn't just one school.

Not just one fountain.

Not just one child.

It was a pattern braided through a mid-sized Southern city: the buildings serving Black and Brown children were the ones where water pressure stuttered, filters clogged, fountains stayed taped shut, and the smallest inconveniences accumulated into a steady erosion of well-being. Children learned to drink less. Teachers learned to compensate more. The system learned to survive its own neglect.

That is the anatomy of inequity—not the one loud failure, but the thousand quiet ones.

Before the Hydration Pilot had a name, before the data and partnerships and policy shifts, before research teams gathered around tables covered in flowmeters and wellness goals, there was simply this:

A child who needed water.

A system that did not deliver it.

And a question that would not leave me alone:

If something this small was failing, what else was collapsing beneath it?

When a regional health system and research partners invited us to examine hydration in schools, I thought we were studying a public health issue. I did not know we were about to uncover the architecture of inequity itself. I did not know water—something so ordinary, so expected—would become the doorway into understanding what children's bodies had been trying to tell us for years.

Hydration was not the problem.

It was the signal.

The symptom.

The origin point.

When a child is dehydrated, the nervous system does what it must to survive: it prioritizes. It shuts down non-essentials—attention, emotion regulation, memory, self-control—because the body is negotiating scarcity. A dehydrated child is not misbehaving; they are trying to function without fuel. And a thirsty school is not underperforming; it is operating below the wellness threshold we never bothered to measure.

We talk about behavior like it's a moral failure.

We talk about learning like it's a choice.

But the body keeps the score long before the test does.

What I saw in those hallways, in those fountains and filters and taped-off spouts, wasn't just neglect. It was a message. A warning. A map of which communities had been allowed to run dry—literally and figuratively.

The Hydration Pilot began with a hypothesis.

But it became a revelation.

When we installed the first hydration stations, the change was immediate. Children who once dragged through the morning sat up straighter. Teachers reported fewer headaches. Fewer nurse visits. Fewer meltdowns. More laughter. More calm. More readiness.

Before the flowmeters gave us numbers, the hallways gave us proof.

And then—when a citywide water system failure hit—everything we had learned became undeniable. The same children who had experienced a drought inside their school walls now faced a drought across their entire city. Public water safety advisories. Systemwide school closures. Empty shelves. Families collecting bottled water like rations. Teachers organizing distribution lines in parking lots.

The pipes failed.

But the people didn't.

The culture we built held even when the infrastructure didn't. Students checked on neighbors. Staff delivered water to families who couldn't leave the house. The same children who once stood helpless at a silent fountain now became leaders in a crisis they never should have had to face.

Equity is not measured by how a system performs when everything is working.

Equity is measured by what survives when everything breaks.

The water crisis didn't expose something new.

It revealed what the children had been saying all along—through dry lips and tired eyes and morning meltdowns we mislabeled as defiance:

You cannot teach a thirsty child.

You cannot discipline a dehydrated nervous system.

You cannot measure brilliance without first meeting basic need.

What began as a hydration project became a lens into the human condition of our schools. It allowed us to see the invisible architecture beneath learning—the conditions that make capacity possible. That is where the Human Equation was born: not in a research lab or policy document, but in the lived experiences of children whose wellness had been treated as optional.

Belonging.

Wellness.

Love.

Equity is not the outcome.

It is the result of honoring these variables at scale.

Origins is not the story of a program. It is the story of how we learned to listen—to bodies, to buildings, to communities, to the quiet truths hiding beneath the obvious ones. It is the story of how care moved from intention to infrastructure. It is the record of the moment before the movement, before we had a name for what we were building and long before we understood what it could become.

If *Refilling the Future* is the manifesto, and *Off the Sidelines* is the mobilization, and *Balancing the Scales* is the restoration, then this—*Origins*—is the excavation.

The digging.

The uncovering.

The remembering.

Education is a living equation, and every system reveals its values through what it chooses to nourish—or neglect.

This is where the Human Equation begins.

Not with victory, but with honesty.

Not with answers, but with attention.

Not with policy, but with people.

Before the pour, there is the thirst.

Before the movement, there is the moment.

And this time, we did not walk past it.

PART I

THE MOMENT BEFORE
THE MOVEMENT

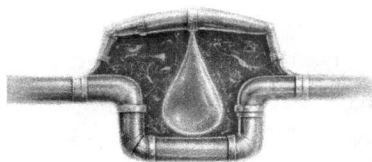

THE FIRST DRIP

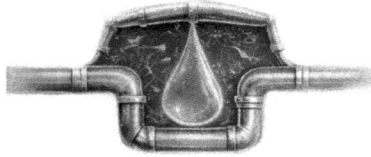

He stood there longer than a child ever should—silent, waiting for water that would not come.

The hallway was already warm, the kind of early-morning heat that settles into old buildings before the sun fully rises. The metal of the fountain felt cool under his fingers, but the spout stayed dry. He pressed the button once. Then again. A third time—slowly, deliberately—as if the building might respond out of obligation.

Nothing.

He didn't look angry. He didn't complain. He looked around—not for help, but for witnesses. Children learn early which disappointments are worth naming and which ones the world has already decided to ignore. This was the second kind.

His lips were cracked. His backpack sagged against his shoulders. He wiped his mouth with the sleeve of his hoodie and walked away, carrying a thirst that no adult noticed because it had become ordinary.

That moment—quiet, unremarkable, easy to miss—was the moment the movement began.

I didn't call it a movement then.

I didn't call it a project.

I didn't even call it a problem.

I just knew something was wrong.

18

A child should not begin the day physiologically depleted before learning even starts. A classroom should not run on empty before it runs on hope. A school should not ration care like it's a privilege.

But for years, we treated small failures as normal. We stepped around broken fountains. We taped handwritten "out of order" signs that stayed up so long they blended into the walls. We carried cases of bottled water to classrooms and called it capacity-building. We spoke about equity in boardrooms while the most basic form of dignity— clean, reliable water—remained inconsistent at best and inaccessible at worst.

No one meant for it to happen.

That's the danger of inequity—it rarely announces itself as cruelty. It arrives as inconvenience. It lingers as delay. And eventually, it settles in as inevitability.

I had been in countless classrooms before that morning. I had sat with teachers who poured themselves into children long after the system stopped pouring back. I had watched leaders stretch budgets thin enough to see through. I had listened to families explain—again and again—that their children were doing their best, even when the system was not.

And still, I had missed the weight of that moment until I saw it repeat.

Not just one school.

Not just one fountain.

Not just one child.

It was a pattern threaded through the city: the schools serving Black and Brown children were the ones where fountains stayed broken longer, filters went unchanged, pressure ran low, and the smallest inconveniences accumulated into chronic depletion.

Children learned to drink less.

Teachers learned to compensate more.

The system learned to survive its own neglect.

That is how inequity operates—not through one loud failure, but through a thousand quiet ones.

Before the pilot had a name, before the data and partnerships and policy shifts, there was simply this:

A child who needed water.

A system that did not deliver it.

And a question that would not leave me alone:

If something this basic is failing, what else is collapsing beneath it?

THE THIRST WE STOPPED SEEING

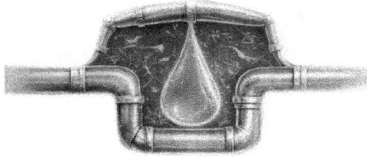

It wasn't just that fountain.

If you walked through certain buildings—usually the ones serving the poorest families, the Blackest neighborhoods, the children whose parents worked the longest hours—you could find the same scenes repeating in different forms:

Fountains taped shut.

Coolers filled once and empty by mid-morning.

Teachers handing out paper cups like ration tickets.

Facilities staff explaining, "We're waiting on parts."

Leaders saying, "We've made a request."

And children asking fewer questions each year because they had learned not to expect answers.

In some classrooms, the routine was almost scripted.

A child would complain of a headache.

The teacher would ask, "Did you drink water today?"

The child would shrug.

The nurse's office would fill before lunch.

Everyone treated it as normal.

Normal is the most dangerous word in education.

Normal is how erosion hides in plain sight.

This wasn't a lack of care. Teachers cared deeply—often at great personal cost. Staff improvised daily. Families trusted the system because trust was sometimes the only resource left.

But when a condition persists long enough, people stop seeing it as a failure and start seeing it as part of the environment.

That's how inequity survives.

It doesn't require cruelty.

It requires accommodation.

WHEN CARE SLIPS OUT OF THE SYSTEM

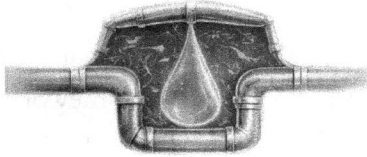

There is a moment in every system when care begins to slip—not because people stop caring, but because survival takes over.

In one elementary school, a teacher kept a case of bottled water under her desk. Not because she wanted to—but because she felt she had to. The fountains were unreliable. Headaches were constant. Students lined up quietly, whispering, "Can I have one?" like they were asking for something forbidden.

She counted the bottles every day, calculating how long they might last.

In another building, a school-based counselor told me she could predict behavioral referrals by the way the hallway felt.

"If the air is heavy," she said, "the afternoon is going to fall apart."

She wasn't talking about temperature.

She was talking about bodies running too close to empty.

This wasn't about motivation.

It wasn't about discipline.

It wasn't about engagement strategies.

It was about biology.

A child can only regulate as well as their body is resourced.

A classroom can only function as well as its environment allows.

A system can only capacity-building what it chooses to maintain.

For years, we asked children to rise above conditions adults had learned to accept. We asked teachers to regulate environments they had no power to repair. We asked schools to produce outcomes without acknowledging the physiological and emotional costs embedded into the day.

This is the hidden truth of education:

We measured everything except the conditions that make learning possible.

And before there was language for it—before the Flow Model, before the Human Equation, before any framework existed—this truth was already present in every headache, every meltdown, every taped-off fountain, every teacher rationing water under a desk.

The crisis wasn't coming.

It was already here.

All it needed was a moment—a child pressing a button on a fountain that refused to respond—for someone to finally say:

This isn't a glitch.

This is the origin point.

And we cannot fix what we refuse to see.

PART II

THE PATTERN

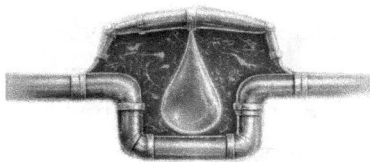

WALKING THE BUILDINGS

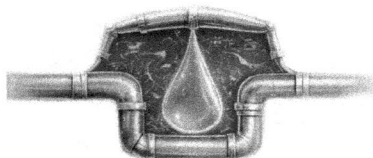

I began walking the buildings without permission, paperwork, or a plan—just a question that wouldn't stop asking me back.

No clipboard. No scheduled assessment. No formal directive. Just footsteps echoing through hallways that smelled of waxed floors, old drywall, and years of deferred decisions. I told myself I was gathering context, learning the heartbeat of each school. But if I'm honest, I was looking for confirmation of something I didn't yet want to name.

The pattern started the way inequity always starts—quiet enough to deny, consistent enough to become normal.

In one school, the fountains ran steady and cold, humming with reliability. In another—only minutes away—the water sputtered, coughed, or didn't come at all. In one building, hydration stations blinked with bright counters that made children proud. In another, filters stayed red so long that students stopped trusting the water entirely.

Same district.

Same city.

Two different realities pretending to be one system.

A facilities staff member in an elementary school serving a historically disinvested community told me, "We've put in the work order. We're waiting on parts." He said it the way someone apologizes for the weather—like the situation existed outside human control.

At another school, a leader gestured toward a broken fountain and said, "It's on the list." When I asked how long it had been on the list, she exhaled.

"Too long," she said. Then, almost reflexively, "But we're making do."

Making do is where inequity learns to survive.

Because making do is both adaptation and surrender. It is the quiet agreement that children will carry what systems refuse to fix.

As I walked, I stopped seeing buildings as structures and started seeing them as bodies. Overworked bodies. Aging bodies. Bodies absorbing decades of underinvestment, shifting priorities, and political neglect. Like the children inside them, these buildings were doing the best they could under conditions they did not choose.

The pattern stopped whispering.

You didn't need a spreadsheet to find inequity.

You just had to follow the pipes—and watch where the flow slowed down.

THE GEOGRAPHY OF THIRST

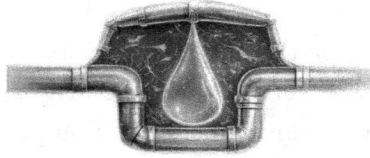

In every city, there are lines you can't see until you live inside them—lines that decide whose water runs cold, whose runs warm, and whose doesn't run at all.

This city was no different.

You could map the thirst without trying. It was already mapped—by history, by housing policy, by which neighborhoods were maintained and which were trained to endure. Schools with the weakest water pressure, the oldest plumbing, and the most unreliable access clustered predictably in the same places: communities shaped by redlining, disinvestment, and long-standing neglect.

The geography of thirst mirrored the geography of inequity.

It didn't matter that all schools operated under the same district or the same policies. Equity does not measure intention. Equity measures outcome.

And the outcome was speaking plainly.

In one school, students approached hydration stations like they approached doors—confident they would open. No hesitation. No waiting. No question about whether the water would be safe, cold, or available.

Ten minutes away, students lined up around a cooler that emptied before the morning was over. Teachers rationed paper cups because they didn't know if facilities would refill it before lunch. Children

28

pressed fountain buttons, watched the slow drip, and walked away disappointed—but not surprised.

The contrast wasn't just physical.

It was emotional.

It shaped expectation.

It shaped trust.

It shaped identity.

When one group of children grows up expecting systems to work and another grows up expecting systems to fail, the system has already written two different futures.

We pretend inequity is abstract.

It is not.

It is the difference between turning a knob and getting water— or pressing a button and hearing silence.

WHAT THE BODY KNOWS BEFORE THE
BOARDROOM DOES

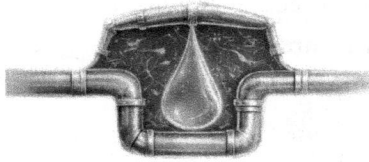

Teachers felt it before anyone named it. They didn't need research language or policy briefs—just one more day of watching children unravel on schedule.

By late morning, the signs appeared. A foot tapping faster. A chair tipping back. Voices sharpening. Eyes glazing. By early afternoon, the entire building carried the same unsettled hum.

Teachers asked the same questions in different ways:

Why are they so tired today?

Why are behaviors spiking after lunch?

Why does everything fall apart at the same time every day?

The boardroom debated performance.

The classroom absorbed physiology.

Water isn't a wellness add-on.

It's a cognitive input.

When hydration is inconsistent, the brain starts cutting corners. Attention falters. Emotional regulation weakens. Memory slips. The nervous system shifts into conservation mode—not because a child doesn't care, but because survival always comes before learning.

A dehydrated child doesn't look like they're struggling physiologically. They look unfocused. Irritable. Defiant. And the system responds accordingly—discipline, removal, correction.

But the body is telling the truth long before the referral does.

One teacher pulled me aside and said, "They're different since the new station went in. Calmer." She said it carefully, like she didn't trust the observation.

Another said, "Afternoons used to be impossible. Now they're… manageable?" She laughed, then stopped. For years, she had blamed herself.

The children hadn't changed.

The conditions had.

The boardroom analyzes outcomes.

The body experiences inputs.

And the body always knows first.

PART III

THE PILOT

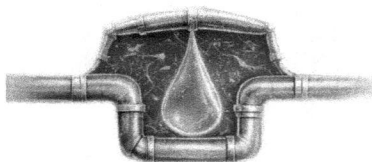

THE BIRTH OF THE PILOT

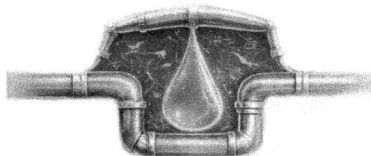

The idea didn't arrive fully formed.

Movements rarely do.

It started as a question in a room full of smart, exhausted people from a regional health system, a pediatric hospital partner, and an urban public school system—people who knew the system intimately and understood its limitations even more intimately.

Someone asked, "Could increasing hydration actually improve student wellness?"

Someone else replied, "We think so."

And then another voice—steady, cautious, hopeful—added, "If we can prove it, we can change everything."

There was no applause, no dramatic moment. Just a table full of nodding heads, the soft hum of an air vent, and a shared sense that we were stepping into something none of us could yet name.

The decision was made: start small.

One school.

One set of hydration stations.

One community willing to see what could happen when dignity became accessible.

On installation day, the sun hit the building in a way it hadn't in years. Facilities staff cleared the hallway. Classroom teachers watched from their doors like parents watching a newborn take a first breath. Students pressed against the walls, wide-eyed, whispering.

The first hydration station blinked to life—cool, stainless steel, steady and sure, its counter set to zero, waiting to be transformed by the hands of children.

A little girl stepped forward, her pink water bottle dented along the side. She placed it under the spout, hesitated, then pressed the button. Water rushed out—cold, clean, abundant.

Her eyes widened.

"That's ours?" she asked.

She didn't say it like a question about ownership.

She said it like a question about worth.

Before anyone collected a single baseline measurement, before the first flowmeter reading, before the formative evaluations and statistical models, the truth revealed itself in the face of a child discovering what she should have always had.

This wasn't about water.

This was about what water represented.

Access.

Care.

Reliability.

Stability.

Possibility.

A school cannot claim to nurture brilliance if it cannot quench thirst.

The pilot didn't start with data.

It started with hope.

WHAT WATER WAKES UP

Classroom teachers noticed it first—not in dramatic shifts but in the tiny recalibrations that only educators with finely tuned emotional intelligence can see.

A student who used to lay his head down by mid-morning now stayed upright through morning meeting.

A girl known for midday meltdowns went a full week without a single incident.

Headaches, once so common they barely registered as complaints, began disappearing.

Nurse visits dropped.

The hum of the hallway changed.

You cannot quantify the sound of a calmer school, but you can feel it.

One teacher told me, "They're... softer." She struggled to find the right words. "Not sleepy. Not quiet. Just... less on edge."

When the body feels safe, the mind becomes available.

Students filled their bottles during transitions, after recess, between math and reading blocks. The hydration station counter ticked upward like a quiet revolution.

A boy proudly announced, "We're up to nine thousand!" Another corrected him, "Nine thousand and sixty-two."

It wasn't about the number.

It was about ownership.

They were measuring their own participation in something bigger than themselves—something that didn't require them to be exceptional, only present.

Then came the afternoon shift.

For years, classroom teachers quietly braced themselves for the post-lunch crash—that window when the nervous system gave out, the classroom rhythm broke, and chaos replaced instruction. But slowly, almost imperceptibly, the crash softened.

Afternoons became survivable.

Then stable.

Then... peaceful.

A school-based counselor told me, "I didn't realize how much of my job was managing dehydration."

A school leader said, half laughing, half crying, "We thought we had a behavior problem. We had a hydration problem."

This wasn't magic.

This was biology.

This was care.

And care, when applied consistently, becomes culture.

WHEN ATTENTION RETURNS, DIGNITY RETURNS

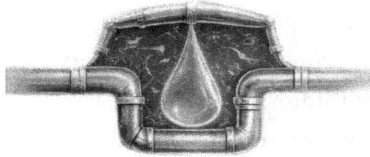

There was a boy in the pilot school whose reputation walked into every room long before he did. Classroom teachers from previous years whispered his name like a warning.

"Be ready," they'd say.

"He's a handful."

Which is code for: *He is carrying more than his body can hold.*

Two weeks into the pilot, his teacher pulled me aside.

"Something's changing," she said.

"He's… here."

"What do you mean?"

"He's with us. He's in his body. He's not spending all day trying to hold himself together."

Hydration didn't fix his trauma.

Hydration didn't replace the capacity-building he deserved.

Hydration didn't heal every wound the world had given him.

But it gave him something he had never consistently had in school:

Capacity.

Capacity to sit.

Capacity to think.

Capacity to breathe.

Capacity to learn.

Capacity to regulate.

Capacity to exist without being at war with his own body.

When capacity returns, dignity returns.

And dignity is the foundation of equity.

What the pilot revealed was bigger than hydration. It exposed a truth that had lived beneath the surface for generations:

Learning is not an academic process.

Learning is a physiological one.

And when schools invest in wellness, even in the smallest ways, the entire ecosystem recalibrates.

Children become more grounded.

Teachers become more effective.

Leaders become more visionary.

Communities become more connected.

The pilot was not just a success.

It was a revelation.

What we thought was a small improvement exposed how often systems respond to the visible outcome while ignoring the invisible cause.

You cannot reform education until you restore the conditions that make learning human.

PART IV

THE SCIENCE BENEATH
THE STORY

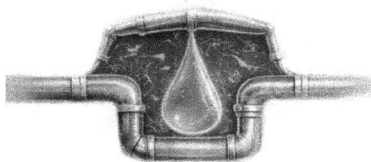

THE HUMAN EQUATION BEGINS FORMING

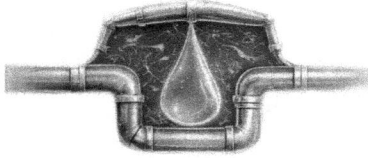

The realization didn't arrive in a meeting or a lab.

It arrived in the space between what I was seeing and what I could no longer unsee.

Every day, I walked into classrooms that felt heavy—not chaotic, not loud, but heavy in a way that settled into the body. The kind of weight you feel before a storm breaks. Teachers spoke more softly, not because students were misbehaving, but because the room itself felt fragile—like any sharp sound might tip it into collapse.

I kept asking myself the same question:

Why do some classrooms feel like breathing is easier than others?

The answer refused to stay hidden.

It wasn't teaching style.

It wasn't curriculum.

It wasn't class size.

It wasn't motivation.

It was conditions.

Invisible, unmeasured, unquestioned conditions shaping how bodies entered learning spaces long before instruction began.

The Human Equation didn't emerge as a theory. It surfaced slowly, like condensation forming on glass—small realizations gathering until a pattern became undeniable.

Wellness shapes capacity.

Capacity shapes behavior.

Behavior determines access to learning.

We had been reading the equation backward.

Children weren't struggling because they lacked skill or will. They were struggling because their bodies were operating under strain. Capacity—this word education had never fully named—was not a mindset or a strategy.

Capacity was biological.

It was bandwidth.

It was regulation.

It was whether a nervous system had enough internal safety to release energy toward learning instead of survival.

We had spent decades fixing outcomes without ever stabilizing origins.

The Human Equation was simply naming what children had already been living.

THE HYDRATION WINDOW

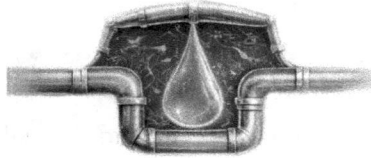

Every school day has a turning point.

It usually arrives quietly—late morning, just before lunch—when the room begins to shift. Focus slips. Frustration rises. The collective nervous system starts to fray.

I began noticing it everywhere.

Feet tapping faster.

Students leaning back in their chairs.

Teachers tightening their voices.

Transitions growing harder.

By early afternoon, the building carried a low-grade unrest.

This wasn't coincidence.

This was physiology.

The nervous system operates like a battery. When hydration is insufficient early in the day, cognitive stamina drains faster. The brain begins conserving energy—pulling conditions away from attention, emotional regulation, impulse control, and working memory.

This is the Hydration Window—the physiological threshold that shapes the entire rest of the day.

Children who enter this window adequately hydrated experience greater stability. They transition more smoothly. They recover more quickly. They remain available for learning.

Children who don't enter it resourced enough shift into survival mode.

Not because they are defiant.

Not because they are disengaged.

But because the body protects itself before it performs.

A dehydrated child is not misbehaving.

A dehydrated child is preserving their brain.

But systems do not recognize preservation.

They punish it.

So the day becomes a cycle of misunderstanding—behavior referrals, discipline, removal from class—while the real cause remains untouched.

We have built entire accountability structures around children's bodies running on empty.

The Hydration Window reveals what schools rarely measure:

When a nervous system is conserving energy to survive, instruction has nowhere to land.

THE WELLNESS THRESHOLD

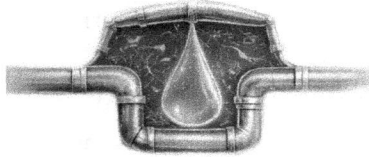

Every body has a limit.

A point where regulation collapses and the brain stops negotiating.

Adults recognize it after long meetings, skipped meals, or chronic stress. Children reach it sooner—faster and more intensely—because their systems are still developing.

The Wellness Threshold is the invisible line where capacity breaks down.

Below it, the body shifts:

Cortisol rises.

Emotional regulation weakens.

Executive function fragments.

Noise feels louder.

Instructions feel heavier.

Frustration overwhelms reasoning.

This is not a failure of will or character.

It is the body responding exactly as designed.

When hydration, nutrition, sleep, sensory safety, or emotional security are compromised, children cross the Wellness Threshold early—and once they do, learning is no longer accessible.

Yet schools rarely respond with restoration.

They respond with discipline.

Children are removed from classrooms. Consequences are issued. Distress is reframed as defiance. And the more dysregulated the environment becomes, the more punitive the system grows.

This cycle exhausts educators, frustrates families, and traumatizes children.

But it begins in the same place every time:

Wellness precedes regulation.

Regulation precedes behavior.

Behavior precedes learning.

Education has been built backward.

And children have been paying the cost with their bodies.

THE CLASSROOM ECOSYSTEM

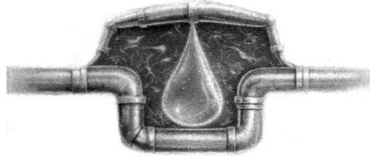

A classroom is not a room.

It is an ecosystem.

Alive. Responsive. Interdependent.

When one nervous system spikes, the room absorbs it.

When one child collapses emotionally, others follow.

When capacity drains collectively, instruction loses its footing.

Teachers feel this instinctively. You can see it in the way they scan the room, adjust their posture, soften their tone. They are reading the ecosystem, not the lesson plan.

This is the truth policy rarely acknowledges:

Regulation is contagious.

Dysregulation is, too.

You cannot ask a teacher to maintain calm in a room full of dysregulated bodies.

You cannot ask children to learn in an environment that destabilizes them.

You cannot demand outcomes where wellness has not been protected.

A school is only as stable as the nervous systems inside it.

The classroom ecosystem made something impossible to ignore:

You cannot fix learning without stabilizing the environment.

You cannot stabilize the environment without restoring wellness. And you cannot restore wellness without understanding the biology beneath behavior.

At this point, the science was no longer separate from the story. The science *was* the story.

PART V

THE ORIGIN OF EQUITY

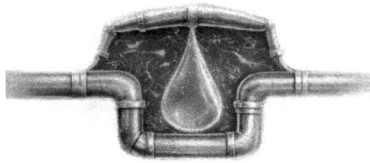

THE WATER THAT REVEALS HISTORY

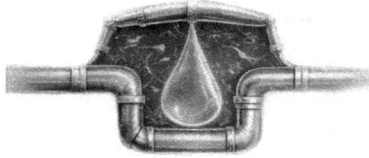

A city tells its story through the parts of itself it allows to crumble.

This city's story lay in its pipes.

You could trace inequity through the veins of the city: the rusted plumbing in neighborhoods ignored for generations, the slow leaks that became permanent fixtures, the infrastructure "updates" that never quite reached the places where Black and Brown children lived and learned.

Nothing about the pattern was accidental.

Nothing about the disparities was new.

Decades ago, maps were drawn—lines of red ink that carved up neighborhoods by race, by income, by perceived value. Those lines did not disappear when the laws changed. They sank underground, into the streets, into the foundations of schools, into the quality of water that flowed—or didn't—into children's cups.

When I walked the buildings, I wasn't just looking at fountains and filters.

I was looking at history.

Some schools had new fill stations, bright and stainless, installed with urgency and pride. Others had fountains that wheezed, coughed, or produced nothing at all. The inequity was so consistent, so structural, that it could have been predicted by zip code.

People talk about equity like it's an abstract policy.

But equity is physical.

It lives in the air children breathe.

It lives in the lights that flicker overhead.

It lives in the temperature of a classroom.

And yes—it lives in the water that runs through a fountain.

Water does not lie.

It reveals.

It reveals which communities were invested in and which were left to *make do*.

It reveals which buildings were maintained and which were merely managed.

It reveals whose comfort mattered and whose safety was optional.

In this city, water drew a map.

And the map told the truth.

THE DIGNITY GAP

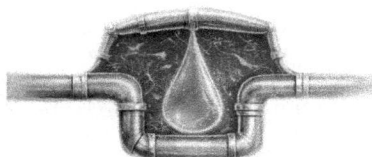

There are gaps we measure in education—achievement gaps, access gaps, funding gaps. But the gap we rarely name, the one shaping everything else, is the **dignity gap**.

Children know when their school is cared for.

They feel it in their bodies.

They know when ceiling tiles are stained.

They know when bathroom doors don't lock.

They know when lights flicker during tests.

They know when fountains stay broken for months.

They know when adults shrug and say, "They're working on it."

Children interpret these signals long before they ever learn to name them:

You deserve less.

Your discomfort is normal.

Your needs are negotiable.

Your environment is an afterthought.

One student told her teacher, "I bring water from home because I don't want to drink school water. It tastes like metal." She said it with resignation, not fear. She had accepted her place in the hierarchy of care.

Another student once said, "The other school has the nice fountains. We don't get those because we're... well..."

He didn't finish the sentence.

He didn't have to.

Dignity is not a perk.

It is a prerequisite for learning.

And when children grow up in buildings that deny them dignity, they internalize that denial. It shapes their relationship to learning, to authority, to the future. A thirsty child is not just missing water. A thirsty child is absorbing a lifetime of messaging about worth.

This is the reality policymakers rarely see:

A child's sense of value is built—or broken—by the mundane.

The fountains.

The filters.

The temperature.

The lighting.

The bathrooms.

The air quality.

The water.

The things adults overlook become the things children cannot escape.

The dignity gap is not measured in test scores.

It is measured in expectations, identity, and hope.

And then—just when the pilot was thriving, when children were finally drinking freely and classroom teachers were witnessing shifts they could barely explain—the city ran dry.

WHEN THE CITY RAN DRY

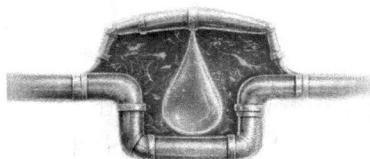

It started with a public water safety advisory.

Just a short alert—a warning, a disruption. But in a place where infrastructure had been held together with patchwork and patience, small warnings rarely stayed small.

Within hours, phones began ringing.

Schools were notified.

Families were told.

Confusion spread.

And suddenly, water—the most basic human necessity—became a crisis.

Parents rushed to grocery stores, only to find shelves empty.

Teachers scrambled to secure bottled water for their students.

School leaders tried to interpret contradictory guidance.

Children asked questions adults didn't yet know how to answer.

School after school closed—not because of snow, not because of testing, not because of staffing shortages—but because the water wasn't safe.

The geographic pattern mirrored everything we had already seen in the pilot: the neighborhoods most historically under-resourced were hit the hardest.

Of course they were.

Infrastructure remembers history.

And yet, something extraordinary happened.

The same children who once stood at broken fountains now stood at distribution lines helping load cases of water into cars. Classroom teachers organized impromptu stations in parking lots. Facilities staff carried pallets like they were carrying their own grandchildren's futures. Communities long labeled "high-need" became the most resilient.

The pipes failed.

But the people didn't.

And it was in that moment—when the city shut down and the schools we were studying lost their most basic resource—that the purpose of the work crystallized.

Hydration was never just about hydration.

Wellness was never just about wellness.

Equity was never just about access.

It was always about infrastructure—physical, emotional, physiological, communal.

If a system cannot protect children during crisis, it was not equitable during stability.

The water crisis didn't expose something new.

It revealed what children had been navigating for years:

Scarcity is not an emergency for everyone.

For some, it is normal.

PART VI

THE RISE OF A MODEL

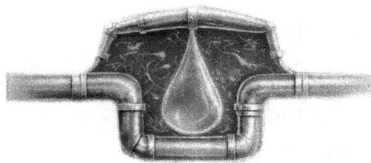

THE FLOW MODEL EMERGES

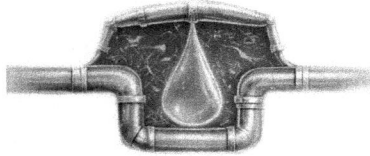

The Flow Model didn't arrive as a sudden breakthrough.

It wasn't born in a meeting or after a single insight.

It emerged through accumulation—the slow gathering of patterns that refused to remain separate.

Every hallway I walked, every classroom I stepped into, every conversation with a classroom teacher, every moment of watching a child try to regulate under impossible conditions—each of these was a fragment.

Individually, they were stories.

Together, they were a system.

The deeper I looked, the clearer it became:

Children weren't responding to individual stressors.

They were responding to an ecosystem.

And ecosystems don't falter because of one variable.

They falter because of the relationships between variables.

So the question shifted.

No longer:

Why is this child struggling?

But:

What conditions consistently precede struggle?

No longer:

Why does behavior spike at certain times?

But:

What changes in the environment occur right before the spike?

No longer:

Why does one classroom feel calm and another feel volatile?

But:

What flows differently between these spaces?

The model began revealing itself—not as a list, but as a pattern language:

Children's bodies respond to internal states.

Internal states respond to the environment.

The environment responds to rhythm and routine.

Rhythm is shaped by relationships.

Relationships are shaped by leadership.

And beneath all of it is the truth:

Schools are living systems.

And learning is only possible when that system flows.

The Flow Model emerged as the first attempt to articulate what schools had been showing us all along:

BODY

Regulation. Hydration. Breath. The internal landscape.

ENVIRONMENT

Air. Light. Temperature. Space. Noise. Infrastructure.

RHYTHM

Transitions. Timing. Pacing. Movement. Recovery moments.

RELATIONSHIP

Safety. Belonging. Trust. Emotional attunement.

LEADERSHIP

The decisions that shape conditions, intentionally or by neglect.

Not five silos.

Not five initiatives.

Five forces that interact constantly, shaping a child's capacity before a single lesson begins.

The Flow Model wasn't a solution.

It was a translation—a way of naming the unseen architecture of every school.

THE CONDITION EQUATION

O nce the Flow Model surfaced, a second truth followed—one that clarified everything we had misunderstood about behavior and learning.

Schools were trying to improve outcomes at the wrong point in the sequence.

We intervene at behavior.

We measure at learning.

But the origin of both is upstream.

The Condition Equation took shape like a formula revealed piece by piece:

Conditions

The physical, emotional, physiological, and environmental context.

Capacity

The nervous system's ability to operate within those conditions.

Behavior

The outward expression of internal capacity.

Learning

The cognitive work only accessible when capacity is available.

This wasn't a theory.

It was an autopsy of every school day.

When conditions were unstable—too hot, too loud, too unpredictable, too thirsty—children's capacity collapsed. And once capacity collapsed, behavior shifted.

And once behavior shifted, learning was no longer possible.

Educators had been trying to manage behavior without addressing capacity, and trying to improve learning without repairing conditions.

The Condition Equation exposed the flaw:

Education has been trying to fix the last step of a process without ever stabilizing the first.

We weren't failing because children couldn't learn.

We were failing because we expected them to learn under conditions adults themselves could not endure.

This was the truth hiding in plain sight, the truth no accountability system was built to acknowledge:

If we do not repair conditions, we cannot build capacity.

If we cannot build capacity, we will always misinterpret behavior.

And if we misinterpret behavior, instruction becomes punishment instead of possibility.

The Condition Equation didn't just explain what was happening.

It revealed why the entire system felt like it was running against itself.

WHY SCHOOLS KEEP FAILING THE ORIGIN POINT

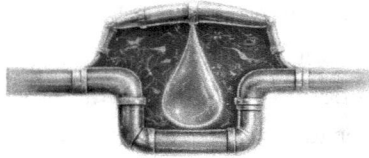

Every institution has an origin point—the place where problems begin before they become visible.

In education, that origin point is conditions.

But schools have been structurally trained to look downstream, not upstream.

So every time a school "fails," leaders and policymakers swarm the outcomes:

Test scores.

Discipline data.

Attendance.

Graduation rates.

Behavior referrals.

We audit the products of distress, not the sources of it.

It is the same misguided pattern everywhere:

We adjust curriculum pacing guides while ignoring the physiological realities of the school day.

We tighten discipline policies instead of increasing wellness infrastructure.

It is a national pattern of treating symptoms instead of origins.

And when you treat symptoms without addressing roots, you create a cycle:

The same behaviors repeat.

The same frustrations return.

The same outcomes persist.

And each generation is blamed for conditions they did not create.

The truth is simple and devastating:

Schools keep failing because we keep fixing the end of the equation instead of the beginning.

If a child is thirsty, stressed, dysregulated, overstimulated, or physically uncomfortable, no amount of curriculum, discipline, or instructional strategy will override their biology.

This is not a failure of children.

It is a failure of design.

A failure of priorities.

A failure of imagination.

The Flow Model and the Condition Equation do not exist to critique schools.

They exist to reveal what schools need:

Environments where bodies can settle,

so minds can open,

so learning can happen,

so equity can be real.

And once a system sees its origin point clearly,

it cannot remain the same.

PART VII

THE TURN TOWARD THE FUTURE

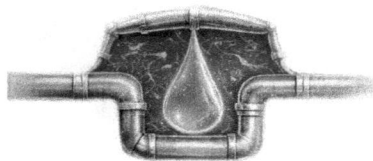

WHEN WELLNESS BECOMES POLICY

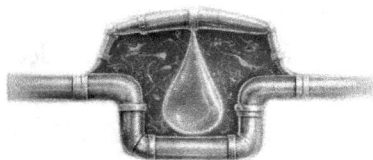

When Wellness Becomes Policy

No one enters education to write policy.

But eventually, every serious effort runs into the same wall:

If care is not written down, it becomes optional.

If equity is not protected, it becomes performative.

If wellness is not embedded into policy, it becomes a luxury only some schools can afford.

The hydration work had already proven what many educators knew intuitively but had never been allowed to say out loud: when conditions change, behavior changes—not because children are compliant, but because their bodies are no longer fighting to survive the day.

Classrooms grew calmer.

Nurse visits declined.

Afternoons stabilized.

Teachers stopped bracing for collapse.

Not because instruction improved, but because physiology did.

What began as a pilot revealed a systems truth: wellness is not supplemental. It is infrastructural. And anything infrastructural must be protected beyond individual goodwill.

So the work had to move upstream.

Water access could no longer depend on which teacher stocked bottles or which administrator pushed hardest. Hydration could no longer be treated as an accommodation instead of a right. Maintenance schedules could no longer be reactive instead of guaranteed.

Policy became the mechanism—not to control classrooms, but to protect conditions.

Water access became expected, not requested.

Hydration breaks became normalized, not exceptional.

Infrastructure maintenance became scheduled, not delayed.

The shift was subtle, but the impact was structural.

The difference between a pilot and a policy is the difference between hope and sustainability.

Pilots rely on champions.

Policy protects children even when champions leave.

THE DATA WE DON'T COLLECT

Education collects data relentlessly.

Attendance.

Behavior referrals.

Test scores.

Benchmarks.

Graduation rates.

We are surrounded by numbers.

And yet, for all this measurement, we routinely ignore the variables that determine whether learning is even possible.

We do not measure hydration.

We do not measure sleep deprivation.

We do not measure sensory overload.

We do not measure emotional safety.

We do not measure building temperature.

We do not measure noise exposure.

We do not measure teacher regulation.

We do not measure classroom stability.

We have built systems fluent in outcomes, but nearly illiterate in the conditions that produce them.

The truth is not that schools lack data.

It's that schools lack *the right data.*

Because the most powerful drivers of learning rarely appear on spreadsheets:

Did the child enter the building regulated?

Did the environment capacity-building that regulation—or erode it?

Did the rhythm of the day preserve capacity—or drain it?

Did relationships reinforce safety—or require self-protection?

Did leadership decisions stabilize the ecosystem—or destabilize it?

We measure what's easy.

We ignore what's essential.

And then we act surprised when outcomes don't change.

The future of education will not be shaped by more testing.

It will be shaped by better listening.

The data we need already live in children's bodies.

We simply have to decide that those signals matter.

THE FIVE WELLS OF STUDENT WELLNESS

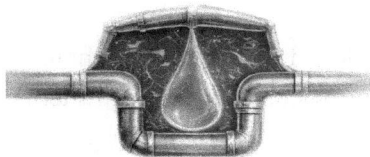

As the work evolved, it became clear that wellness could not be treated as a single initiative or program.

It had structure.

It had domains.

It had roots.

The Five Wells of Student Wellness are not add-ons. They are not environmental shifts. They are not optional capacity-buildings layered on top of "real" learning.

They are prerequisites.

Foundational conditions that nourish capacity before learning ever begins.

Physical Wellness

Hydration. Nutrition. Sleep. Movement. Sensory balance.

The biological baseline.

Emotional Wellness

Safety. Belonging. Regulation. Validation.

The internal climate.

Environmental Wellness

Air. Light. Temperature. Space. Sound.

The external conditions learning depends on.

Relational Wellness

Trust. Warmth. Cultural affirmation. Consistency.

The connective tissue of learning.

Cognitive Wellness

Predictability. Rhythm. Pacing. Recovery.

The brain's operating environment.

A system cannot claim to be equitable if even one of these wells is running dry.

We cannot ask children to think while their bodies are in distress.

We cannot demand focus while environments destabilize them.

We cannot preach rigor while ignoring regulation.

The future of education is not about delivering more content.

It is about protecting the conditions that allow content to matter.

WHEN CARE BECOMES CULTURE

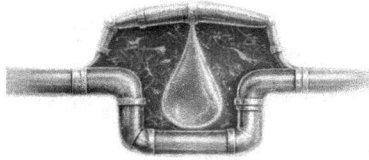

There was a moment—months after the pilot, after the crisis, after the frameworks had names—when I walked into a school and felt something unfamiliar.

Quiet.

Not silence.

Quiet.

The kind that signals a nervous system finally has room to breathe.

Students refilled water bottles without asking.

Teachers transitioned calmly between activities.

A counselor led a movement break in the hallway.

Lighting had softened.

The building felt coordinated rather than reactive.

It wasn't perfect.

It wasn't polished.

But it was intentional.

That's what culture is: the accumulation of choices that shape an environment even when no one is watching.

When wellness becomes culture:

Teachers stop blaming themselves for what was never their fault.

Students stop internalizing distress as failure.

Leaders stop managing crises and start protecting conditions.

Families stop feeling powerless and start feeling included.

Schools stop surviving.

They begin to breathe.

When care becomes culture, learning stops being transactional. It becomes relational.

And equity stops being rhetorical.

It becomes real.

This is the turn toward the future—not through promises, but through design.

Not overnight transformation, but sustained protection of what bodies need to function.

Once a system understands this, it cannot return to ignorance.

The work becomes clear.

PART VIII
THE BEGINNING

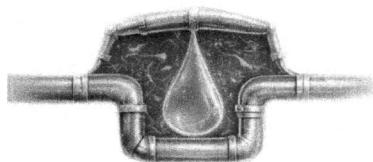

THE HUMAN EQUATION

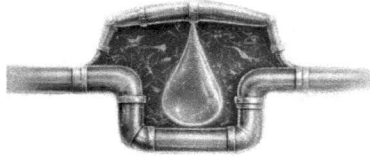

There is a point in every story where the truth stops whispering and begins to speak plainly.

For months—maybe years—the pieces had been sitting in front of us: behavior spikes, hydration scarcity, classroom dysregulation, inequitable infrastructure, tired teachers, exhausted children, over-whelmed buildings. Each one seemed separate until the work forced them into the same frame.

And once aligned, the truth was undeniable:

Education is not driven by curriculum.

It is driven by conditions.

Students do not learn because we teach well.

They learn because their bodies feel safe enough to release the energy required to learn.

Teachers do not thrive because they receive more training.

They thrive because the system gives them the conditions to use the training they already have.

Equity does not fail because we lack strategies.

Equity fails because we keep trying to fix outcomes while ignoring origins.

The Human Equation clarified the structure beneath it all:

Belonging + Wellness + Love → Capacity → Learning → Equity

Not as metaphor.

As physiology.

As psychology.

As history.

As lived reality.

Belonging regulates the nervous system.

Wellness stabilizes it.

Love reinforces it.

Capacity emerges from it.

Learning grows through it.

Equity becomes possible because of it.

Every part of the Human Equation is human.

No part is optional.

Children are not variables to be solved.

They are human beings who require humanity to flourish.

The Human Equation did not replace the system.

It revealed the system beneath the system—the one operating in every hallway, every classroom, every child's body, whether we acknowledge it or not.

And once you see it, it changes everything.

BEFORE THE POUR

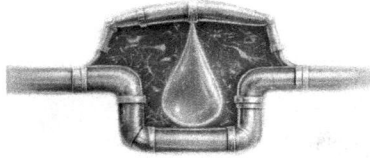

Months after the pilot began, and weeks after the water crisis receded, I found myself back in a familiar hallway—the same hallway where a silent fountain had set this journey in motion.

But now the fountain was gone.

In its place stood a hydration station humming with stability, its digital counter glowing like a heartbeat.

A child walked up, pressed the button, and watched their bottle fill.

No flinch.

No hesitation.

No doubt that it would work.

They simply expected it to.

That expectation—the belief that basic needs will be met—is the foundation of dignity.

They took a sip, wiped their mouth with the back of their hand, and walked away without ever knowing that months earlier, another child had stood in that same spot learning a very different lesson.

That's how change works.

When it's real, it erases the memory of what came before.

But I remembered.

I remembered the button that produced nothing.

I remembered the teacher rationing bottles.

I remembered the cooler running dry before the morning was over.

I remembered the crisis that exposed the truth we had been living all along.

And I realized something:

The movement didn't begin with the installation of a hydration station.

It didn't begin with a research proposal or a policy shift.

It didn't begin with data.

It began with a moment.

A child.

A forgotten fountain.

A truth that demanded to be seen.

Before the pour, there is always the thirst.

And before the movement, there is always the moment when we decide that thirst is no longer acceptable.

That is the origin of everything.

THE BLUEPRINT FOR REFILLING THE FUTURE

By the time *ORIGINS* reaches this point, the reader has walked the journey with you—through the buildings, through the data, through the crisis, through the revelation, through the models.

Now they understand:

We cannot reform what we refuse to rehumanize.

We cannot rehumanize what we refuse to see.

The blueprint is simple—but not easy:

Build systems that nourish the body.

Build environments that stabilize the mind.

Build rhythms that honor the nervous system.

Build relationships that reaffirm dignity.

Build leadership that protects the conditions children depend on.

Build equity through infrastructure, not intention.

This is not the end of the work.

It is the beginning of the language for the work.

ORIGINS is the excavation—the uncovering of truths long buried beneath tradition, policy, and assumption.

The next book will ask a different question:

Now that we know the origins, what will we build?

But for now, the message is clear:

A better system is not only possible.

It is already emerging in every classroom where care becomes culture, where wellness becomes policy, and where children walk in expecting what they should have always had:

Water.

Safety.

Belonging.

Love.

A chance to learn with a body that is ready.

This is not the conclusion.

It is the invitation.

The future is not refilled through programs.

It is refilled through people—one condition, one moment, one act of care at a time.

THE BEGINNING

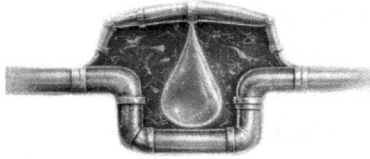

The hallway is quiet.
   The counter blinks.
   A bottle fills.
   A child laughs softly—just enough sound to echo.
   And you realize:
   This is not a story about water.
   This is a story about worth.
   This is not the finale of a project.
   It is the opening chapter of a movement.
   This is not where the work ends.
   It is where the Human Equation begins.
   And now—finally—so does the future.

ACKNOWLEDGMENTS

This book exists because of people who showed up—often quietly, often without recognition—when systems did not.

I am grateful to the educators who opened their classroom doors and trusted me with what they were seeing and feeling, even when they did not yet have language for it. Your honesty, exhaustion, intuition, and care shaped every page of this work. You carried children on days when the system could not, and you did it with a courage that rarely makes headlines.

To the students whose bodies told the truth before the data ever did—thank you. You were never the problem. You were the signal. Your thirst, your fatigue, your resilience, and your brilliance revealed what adults had learned to overlook. This book is written in deep respect for what you endured and what you taught us simply by being present.

To the school leaders, facilities staff, nurses, counselors, and capacity-building personnel who understood that learning depends on conditions long before outcomes—your work mattered more than you may ever know. You reminded us that infrastructure is not abstract. It is lived. It is felt. And it is carried by people every day.

I am thankful for the research partners and health professionals who were willing to ask uncomfortable questions, to look upstream, and to follow the evidence wherever it led. Your commitment to interdisciplinary thinking made it possible to bridge story and science without sacrificing either.

To the families who trusted schools to care for their children under conditions that were often insufficient—your faith, advocacy, and perseverance deserve far more than acknowledgment. They deserve systems that honor that trust.

Finally, this work would not exist without the mentors, colleagues, and loved ones who reminded me—again and again—that naming the truth is an act of care. Thank you for holding space, challenging assumptions, and believing that a more human system is not only necessary, but possible.

This book is for all of you.

GLOSSARY OF CORE TERMS

The Human Equation

A framework that recognizes learning as the product of belonging, wellness, and love operating together to create capacity, which makes learning and equity possible.

Capacity

The nervous system's available bandwidth to regulate, engage, and learn. Capacity is biological, not motivational.

Conditions

The physical, emotional, physiological, environmental, and relational factors that shape a student's ability to access learning.

The Flow Model

A systems framework identifying five interacting forces—Body, Environment, Rhythm, Relationship, and Leadership—that shape how learning ecosystems function.

The Condition Equation

A sequence illustrating how Conditions influence Capacity, which shapes Behavior, making Learning possible or inaccessible.

Hydration Window

A critical period early in the school day when hydration levels significantly impact cognitive stamina, emotional regulation, and behavior.

Wellness Threshold

The point at which unmet physiological or emotional needs cause a child's capacity to collapse, making regulation and learning inaccessible.

Five Wells of Student Wellness

The foundational domains required for learning:

- Physical
- Emotional
- Environmental
- Relational
- Cognitive

Dignity Gap

The disparity in how environments communicate worth, safety, and care to students through infrastructure, maintenance, and daily conditions.

Classroom Ecosystem

The dynamic, interdependent system created by the nervous systems, relationships, and environmental conditions within a learning space.

CLOSING NOTE

This book is not a conclusion.

It is a lens.

If it sharpens your attention to the conditions around you—in classrooms, hallways, offices, or systems—then it has done its work.

The future will not be shaped by what we intend, but by what we build, protect, and refuse to ignore.

ABOUT THE AUTHOR

Kevin A. Starlings is an educator, systems thinker, and advocate whose work centers the relationship between wellness, equity, and learning. He has spent years working alongside students, educators, families, and school systems to understand how conditions—physical, emotional, environmental, and relational—shape capacity long before outcomes appear.

His work bridges lived experience and research-informed practice, focusing on how bodies move through educational systems and what those systems reveal through the care they provide—or withhold. Through partnerships across education, health, and community spaces, he has contributed to the development of frameworks that help schools move upstream, addressing origins rather than symptoms.

Starlings is the creator of the Human Equation framework and related models that reframe learning as a physiological and relational process, not solely an academic one. His work emphasizes dignity as infrastructure and argues that equity becomes possible only when human needs are treated as foundational rather than supplemental.

He lives and works in Richmond, Virginia and remains committed to building systems where care is not optional, wellness is not a privilege, and every child enters learning spaces with their humanity intact.

www.ingramcontent.com/pod-product-compliance
Lightning Source LLC
Chambersburg PA
CBHW050656270326
41927CB00012B/3051